The Drug Awareness Library™

Danger:
DRUGS AND YOUR FRIENDS

E. Rafaela Picard

The Rosen Publishing Group's
PowerKids Press™
New York

Published in 1997 by The Rosen Publishing Group, Inc.
29 East 21st Street, New York, NY 10010

First Edition

Book Design: Erin McKenna

Photo Illustrations: Cover by Seth Dinnerman; p. 7 © Caroline Wood/International Stock; all other photo illustrations by Seth Dinnerman.

Picard, E. Rafaela.
    Danger: drugs and your friends / E. Rafaela Picard.
        p.   cm. — (The drug awareness library)
    Includes index.
    Summary: Introduces the topic of illegal drugs, explaining what they are, how they cause harm, why some people use them, and how to say no.
    ISBN 0-8239-5049-2
    1. Youth—Drug use—United States—Juvenile literature. 2. Drug abuse—United States—Prevention—Juvenile literature. [1. Drugs.] I. Title. II. Series.
    HV5824.Y68S46 1996
    362.29'17'0973—dc21   96-39267
                                                                  CIP
                                                                   AC

Manufactured in the United States of America

Contents

What Is a Friend?   **5**

Friends and Peer Pressure   **6**

What Is a Drug?   **9**

Why People Use Drugs   **10**

The Effects of Drugs   **13**

Hurting People   **14**

Dealers Are Not Friends   **17**

Be Smart   **18**

Helping a Friend   **21**

Taking Care of Yourself   **22**

Glossary   **23**

Index   **24**

What Is a Friend?

A friend is someone you like and spend time with. She is someone you share secrets with, and someone you trust. She cares about you. She is glad when you are happy. She helps you feel better when you are sad.

Your friends **influence** (IN-floo-ents) you. You care about what they think. That is why it is important to choose your friends carefully. A true friend really cares about you. Someone is not a true friend if she tries to make you do things that can hurt you, such as try drugs.

◀ It is important to choose friends who really care about you.

Friends and Peer Pressure

Negative peer pressure (NEG-uh-tiv PEER PREH-sher) is when someone around your age tries to get you to do something that is bad or harmful. Someone who is not a true friend may use negative peer pressure to try to get you to use drugs or drink alcohol. If you don't do it, he may say that you're not cool or that you're scared. Someone who does this is not a friend. A friend knows that using drugs and alcohol can hurt you. A friend won't push you to do something harmful.

A true friend wants you to do positive, or good, things. ▶

What Is a Drug?

A drug is something a person takes to change the way she thinks, acts, or feels. Some drugs, called medicines, can help your body heal when you are sick. Your parent or your doctor may give you medicine when you are not feeling well.

Other drugs, such as cocaine, heroin, crack, and marijuana, can hurt people who use them. These drugs are dangerous. But some people use them anyway. It is against the law to buy, sell, or use these drugs.

◀ Your doctor may give you medicine to help you get well when you are sick.

9

Why People Use Drugs

Many people try drugs or drink alcohol because their friends use them. Some people use drugs because they feel sad or lonely. They may think that drugs will help them fit in or be **popular** (POP-yoo-ler). Other people use drugs as a way to forget their worries. But when their "**high**" (HY) goes away, they feel even worse. Using drugs or drinking alcohol doesn't make a person popular or help her fit in or solve her problems. It just causes more problems.

10

Many kids try drugs or alcohol ▶
because their friends use them.

The Effects of Drugs

Drugs can make a person feel high and forget her problems for a while. But drugs hurt a person's body and mind. Some drugs can make a person feel sad or very afraid. Other drugs make a person see, hear, and feel things that are not real. Drugs can make someone throw up, feel shaky, or become **violent** (VY-uh-lent). And some drugs can kill a person the first time he uses them. Drugs are dangerous. It is against the law to use most drugs.

◀ A person never knows how a drug will make her feel. It may make her sick to her stomach.

Hurting People

People who use drugs may think they are cool, but they are hurting themselves. A person who uses drugs can become **addicted** (uh-DIK-ted). That means that he **craves** (KRAYVZ) drugs and thinks he cannot live without them. When someone is addicted to drugs, he is not himself anymore. His life centers on drugs. He may steal from his family or friends. He may even kill someone to get money to buy more drugs.

A person who is addicted to drugs may steal money ▶ from his family or friends to buy more drugs.

Dealers Are Not Friends

People who sell drugs are called **drug dealers** (DRUG DEE-lerz). They make money by finding new people to buy drugs from them. They may give away drugs to people, including their friends. Drug dealers want these people to become addicted to the drugs. The new addicts will then buy drugs from the drug dealers. Drug dealers may seem friendly. But they care more about making money than they do about the people they sell drugs to. Drug dealers are not good friends.

◀ Drug dealers sometimes hang around school playgrounds looking for new drug users.

Be Smart

If you don't use drugs, be smart and don't start. If you do use drugs, ask yourself why. Do you use drugs to fit in? Do you use drugs to get away from problems in your life?

If you use drugs, you can find better ways to deal with problems in your life. You can talk about the problems with an adult you trust, such as a parent, teacher, or counselor. They can help you stop using drugs. Don't be afraid to ask for help. Everybody needs help sometimes.

Find an adult that you trust and talk to him. ▶

Helping a Friend

You may have a friend who is hurting herself by using drugs. You may want to help her. One way to help is by telling your friend that you care about her. Tell her that you are afraid that her drug use is hurting her. Tell her she can talk to an adult she trusts about her drug use. Offer to go with her for help.

Your friend may be happy that you offered your help. Or she may get angry at you. But you will know that you did your best to help her. You will know that you are a true friend.

◀ True friends stick together and help each other out.

Taking Care of Yourself

It is important to take care of yourself. **Respect** (ree-SPEKT) yourself. That means that what *you* think is right and wrong means more to you than what your friends think. It's a good idea to have friends who don't use drugs. But if one of your friends does offer you drugs, say "No." A real friend won't pressure you to do something that you don't want to do. A real friend will respect your choice not to use drugs.

Glossary

addicted (uh-DIK-ted) Not able to control your use of a drug.

crave (KRAYV) Need or want badly.

drug dealer (DRUG DEE-ler) Someone who sells illegal drugs.

high (HY) A false feeling of happiness when using a drug.

influence (IN-floo-ents) The effect a person or thing has on another.

negative peer pressure (NEG-uh-tiv PEER PREH-sher) When people your age push you to do something you don't want to do.

popular (POP-yoo-ler) Having many friends.

respect (ree-SPEKT) To think highly of someone.

violent (VY-uh-lent) Acting with hurtful force.

Index

A
alcohol, 6, 10

D
doctor, 6
drugs, 6
    addiction, 14
    cravings, 14
    dealers, 17
    effects, 13
    reasons why
        people use,
        10
    selling, 17
    users, 6

F
friends, 5, 6, 22
    helping, 21
    giving drugs to,
        17
    using drugs, 10

H
"high," feeling,
    10, 13
help, asking for,
    18

M
medicine, 9

N
negative peer
    pressure, 6

P
popular, being, 10

R
respect, 22

V
violence, 13